Ginger

Pupil's Book 3

Allgemeine Ausgabe – Neubearbeitung
Lehrwerk für Englisch ab Klasse 3

Überarbeitet von
Kerstin Caspari-Grote, Ina Grandt,
Ulrike Kraaz, Claudia Neuber,
Christel Simon, Ines Völtz
auf der Grundlage der Ausgabe
von Birgit Hollbrügge und Ulrike Kraaz

Cornelsen

Contents

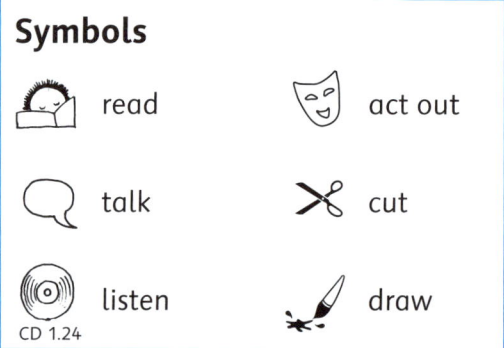

Symbols

read		act out	
talk		cut	
listen	CD 1.24	draw	

English words

 1 Talk.

 2 Read.

popcorn
sandwich
jeans
toast
poster
T-shirt
computer
e-mail

That's English
Cowboy, mountain bike and shop.
That's English!
Popcorn, in-line skates and stop.
That's English!
Scooter, skateboard, king of pop.
That's English!

Families

 1 Talk.

Linda   John   Lucy   Captain Storm

Jenny   Tom

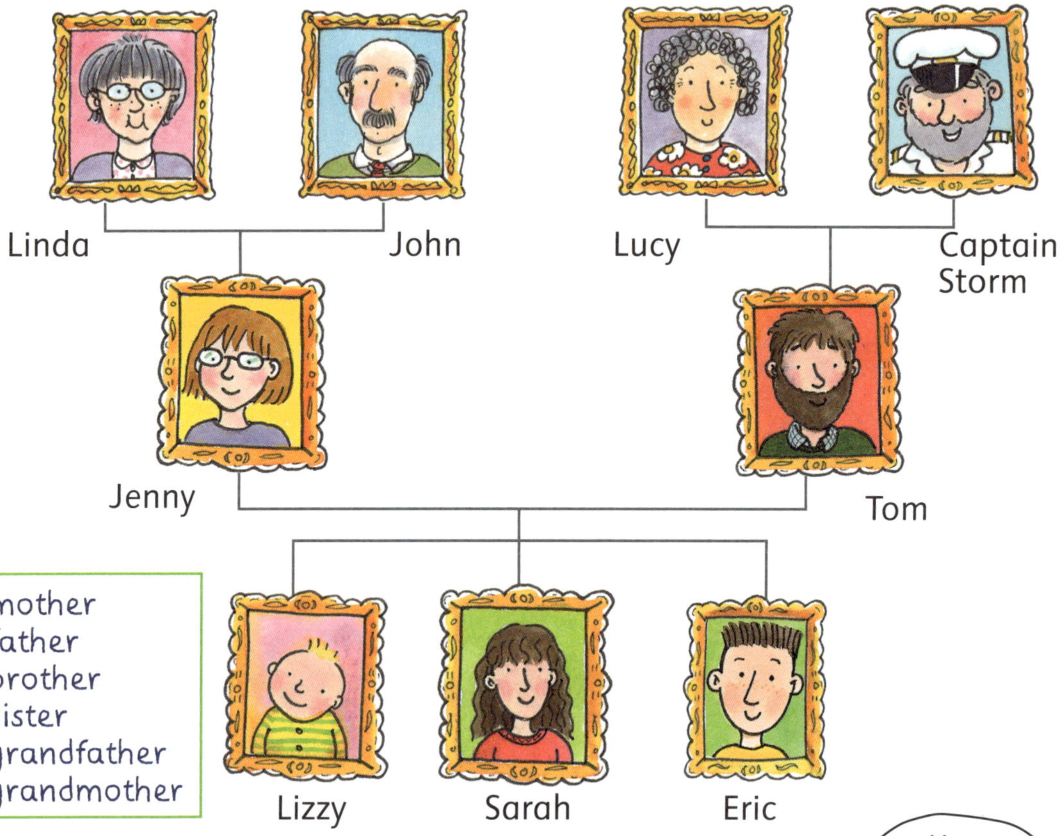

mother
father
brother
sister
grandfather
grandmother

Lizzy   Sarah   Eric

 2 Read.

Some families

Some families are big.
Some families are small.
But I love my family best of all.

Have you got a brother?

Have you got a sister?

Eine Familie beschreiben; einen Reim sprechen und lesen ▸ S. 60

Meeting the crew

1 Talk.　　2 Read.　　3 Act out.

Dr Heal

Debbie Jones

Captain Storm

Colin Baker

Ravi Mehta

Hello, children. Welcome aboard!

Hello, Ravi. Here are my friends!

Ginger's cabin

 1 Talk.

 2 Listen.

CD 1.19

Einen Hörtext verstehen; sagen, wo sich verschiedene Gegenstände in der Kabine befinden ▸ S. 69 f.

Telephone calls

💬 **1** Talk. 💿 CD 1.21 **2** Listen.

Captain Storm   Debbie Jones   Ravi Mehta

Hello?

Canada

Great Britain

USA

India

South Africa   Australia

Dr Heal   Ginger   Colin Baker

Orange Island

Breakfast on board

 **1** Listen and read.   **2** Act out.

CD 1.24

1 It's Monday morning.

2 It's Tuesday morning.

Einen Dialog verstehen und vorlesen, Frühstücksszenen nachspielen ▸ S.81

3 It's Wednesday morning.

4 It's Thursday morning.

5 It's Friday morning.

Sandwich game

 1 Talk.

2 Play the game.

What do you like on your sandwich?

Sandwiches
1. tuna
   lettuce
2. ham
   cheese

Start

1 2 3 4

15 14 13 12

16

17 18 19

Sam...

Ein Bild beschreiben und Sandwichbeläge benennen, ein Spiel spielen ▶ S. 89 f.

's Sandwiches

Pete's ice cream stand

1 Talk.

2 Read.

Spotlight Landeskunde: English breakfast

1 Talk.

Do you like baked beans for breakfast?

mushrooms

toast

fried eggs

baked beans

sausages

tea

fried bacon

Ginger's island game

1 Talk. **2** Play the game.

Put
your cards
here

Take
a
card

Take
a
card

→ Go
forward
3 steps

↑ Go
forward
4 steps

Take
a
card

Go
back ↓
4 steps

Take
a
card

Take
a
card

Go
→ back
3 steps

START

Go back steps

Take a card

Take a card

Take a card

Go back 4 steps

Finish

Take a card

Take a card

← Go forward 3 steps

Take a card

Go forward 3 steps

Take a card

Go ↑ back 2 steps

Go ↓ forward 3 steps

Go ← forward 3 steps

Circus Island

Five big elephants

  1 Read.   **2** Act out.

Five big elephants – oh, what a sight.

Swinging their trunks from left to right.

Four are the followers and one is the king.

They all walk around in the circus ring.

Einen Reim lesen und nachspielen ▸ S. 107

Tim, the tightrope walker

 Talk.

 Listen and read.

CD 1.46

Ringmaster: Ladies and gentlemen, here's Tim, the tightrope walker.

Tim: I'm Tim, the tightrope walker.
Five steps forward: one, two, three, four, five.
Five steps back: five, four, three, two, one.

Ringmaster: Thank you, Tim.
Please give Tim a big hand.

Tim: Thank you, ladies and gentlemen.

Spotlight Landeskunde: Sports and games at school

1 Talk.

skipping

playing clapping games

| Start |
| Assembly |
| Lesson 1 |
| Break |
| Lesson 2 |
| Lunch / Break |
| Lesson 3 |
| Lesson 4 |
| End of School |

I like coffee, I like tea, I want Jim to jump with me!

playing hopscotch

dancing

playing hockey

playing cricket

Schulsportarten und Pausenaktivitäten in Großbritannien kennenlernen und sich darüber austauschen ▶ S. 119

What's the weather like?

1 Talk about the weather.

Dr Heal's photos

 1 Listen.

CD 1.51

 2 Talk.

Einen Hörtext verstehen und Bilder beschreiben ▸ S. 126

In the jungle

1 Listen.   **2** Play the game.

CD 1.52

a red butterfly and
a yellow butterfly

a chameleon
in a tree

a bird

a red flower and
a blue flower

I like mud

 **1** Listen. Read.

CD 2.05

I like mud.
I like it on my clothes.
I like it on my fingers.
I like it on my toes.

 2 Read. Right or wrong?

1 There are eleven trees.

2 There's a red snake.

3 There are five birds.

4 Ginger has got mud on his T-shirt.

5 There's a yellow and green butterfly.

6 Dr Heal is in the picture.

Über ein Bild sprechen, einen Reim lesen ▸ S. 131

Ginger's photos

 **1** Listen.

CD 2.09

 **2** Read.

There's a butterfly on my toe.

There's a bird and a snake in the photo.

There's a chameleon in the tree.

Spotlight Landeskunde: Photos from Great Britain

1 Listen and talk.

1 Ben Nevis

2 Nessie in Loch Ness

3 English roses

4 On the beach (Cornwall)

5 Stonehenge

8 Robin Red Breast

7 Peak District

6 The River Thames

Landeskundliche Informationen anhand eines Hörtextes verstehen ▶ S.142

Debbie calls for help

 **1** Listen.

CD 2.15

 2 Talk.

Robot City

 **1** Talk.

Ein Bild beschreiben, über den eigenen Wohnort sprechen ▸ S. 148

Professor Bit's house

 **1** Talk.

Robot in the bedroom

  1 Read.

Robot in the bedroom,
make my bed.
– No, no.
Off you go.

Robot in the kitchen,
make my toast.
– No, no.
Off you go.

Robot in the bathroom,
wash my hair.
– No, no.
Off you go.

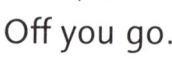 **2** Talk.

Einen Chant lesen, neue Strophen formulieren ▸ S. 155 f.

Spotlight Landeskunde: My home is my castle

 **1** Read and talk. **2** Listen.

CD 2.34

a cottage

a terraced house

a semi-detached house

a block of flats

a palace

Do you live in a house or in a flat?

John

Kate

Lisa

The Queen

My house is not big,
my house is not small.
Kitchen and living room,
bedroom, bathroom, a hall.
A garden, a balcony,
a swimming pool, too.
I like my dream house!
And what about you?

Landeskundliche Informationen anhand eines Hörtextes verstehen und Bilder zuordnen, einen Reim lesen ▶ S. 163 f.

twenty-nine   29

Let's have a party

 **1** Talk.

  2 Listen.

CD 2.38

Oh, no!
Can you help me?

Good idea!
We can help you,
Prince Charming.

Let's help
the prince.

Please come to my
party

When: Sunday
8 o'clock
Where: the castle

Prince
Charming

Ein Bild beschreiben, einen Dialog verstehen ▸ S. 170

I paint my fingernails

 1 Talk.  **2** Read.

> I paint my fingernails
> yellow, white and blue.
> Orange, green and red and brown.
> Dwarfs – I love you.

Is this your shoe?

 Talk.

 CD 2.52 Listen.

Is this your
shoe?

No,
it isn't.

Let's go,
Ravi.

I love you.

Einen Hörtext verstehen, Bilder einer Geschichte sortieren ▸ S. 181 f.

A storybook

1 Talk. Make your book.

Spotlight Landeskunde: The Royal Family

 **1** Talk.

The Queen

Prince Charles and Camilla

Prince William and Kate

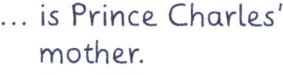

> … is Prince Charles' mother.
> … has 775 rooms and 78 bathrooms.
> … is Prince William's stepmother.
> … is Prince William's brother.
> … is Prince Harry's father.
> … likes dogs.

Prince Harry

Buckingham Palace

The Queen's dogs

 **2** Make a pop-up card.

1) Fold.

2) Cut.

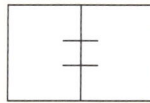
3) Open.

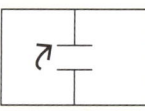
4) Pull out.

5) Fold.

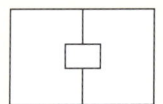
6) Open.

7) Colour and glue.

Landeskundliche Informationen verstehen, Bild und Text zuordnen, eine Pop-up-Karte basteln ▸ S. 185

Birthday

 **1** Talk. **2** Read.

January • February • March • April • May • June • July •
August • September • October • November • December

 **3** Talk.

Über Geburtstage sprechen ▸ S. 189 f.

Halloween

  1 Talk.

  2 Read.

Trick or treat!
Smell my feet!
Give me something
good to eat!

Knock, knock, knock!
Trick or treat!
Do you want some candy
or an apple to eat?

Bilder beschreiben und Unterschiede finden, Reime lesen ▶ S. 191 f.

Christmas

 1 Talk.

Christmas dinner with crackers and paper hats •
Christmas stockings • Christmas presents • Father Christmas

Word list

A

across über
act Nummer bei einer
    Aufführung
action Aktivität, Handlung
address Adresse
airport Flughafen
animal Tier
animal trainer
    Dompteur/in
apple Apfel
April April
arm Arm
August August
Australia Australien
autumn Herbst

B

back hinterer Teil,
    Rücken, zurück
*****bacon** Speck
bad böse, schlecht
bag Tasche
*****baked beans** weiße
    Bohnen in Tomatensauce
banana Banane
basket Korb
bathroom Badezimmer
*****beach** Strand
bear Bär
beautiful schön
bed Bett
bedroom Schlafzimmer
big groß
bike Fahrrad
bird Vogel
birthday Geburtstag
bitter bitter
black schwarz
blue blau
boat Boot
body Körper
book Buch
boy Junge
bread Brot
breakfast Frühstück
broken kaputt
brother Bruder
brown braun
bus Bus

bus stop Bushaltestelle
butterfly Schmetterling

C

cabin Kabine
camera Fotoapparat
can können
Canada Kanada
candy Bonbon, Süßigkeit
cap Mütze
car Auto
car park Parkplatz
card Karte
carry tragen
castle Schloss
chair Stuhl
chameleon Chamäleon
child, children Kind,
    Kinder
*****cave** Höhle
cheese Käse
chocolate Schokolade
Christmas Weihnachten
circus Zirkus
circus act Zirkusnummer
city Stadt
clap klatschen
*****clapping** Klatschen
clean sauber,
    saubermachen
climb down herabsteigen
climb up hinaufsteigen
clock (Stand-)Uhr
close schließen
clothes Kleidung
cloudy bewölkt
clown Clown
coat Mantel
cold kalt
coloured pencil Buntstift
come kommen
computer Computer
computer game
    Computerspiel
cornflakes Cornflakes
cracker Knallbonbon
*****cricket** Kricket
crocodile Krokodil
cucumber Gurke
*****cup** Tasse

D

daffodil Narzisse
*****dance** tanzen
*****dancing** Tanzen
dangerous gefährlich
dark dunkel
dear liebe/r
December Dezember
deck Deck
desk Schreibtisch
dinner Abendessen
*****dog** Hund
door Tür
down hinunter
*****dragon** Drache
dream Traum
dress Kleid
drink Getränk
dwarf Zwerg

E

ear Ohr
eat essen
egg Ei
elephant Elefant
England England
eye Auge

F

face Gesicht
fairy Fee
fairy tale Märchen
fall fallen
family Familie
father Vater
Father Christmas
    Weihnachtsmann
favourite Lieblings-
February Februar
feet Füße
finger Finger
fixed repariert
flap auf und ab bewegen
flower Blume
foggy neblig
food Essen
foot Fuß
forward vorwärts
freckles Sommersprossen
Friday Freitag
*****fried** gebraten

friend Freund/in
fruit Obst
fun Spaß, Scherz

G

game Spiel
garden Garten
Germany Deutschland
ghost Gespenst
girl Mädchen
give geben
glass Glas
glue Klebstoff, kleben
go gehen
good gut
goodbye auf Wiedersehen
grandfather Großvater
grandmother Großmutter
grapefruit Grapefruit
grass Gras
great großartig
green grün

H

hair Haar
*****hall** Diele, Flur
ham Schinken
hammock Hängematte
hand Hand
happy glücklich
has got hat
hat Hut, Mütze
have got habe/n
head Kopf
help helfen
high hoch
*****hockey** Hockey
home Haus, Heim
*****hopscotch** Himmel-und-
  Hölle-Hüpfspiel
horse Pferd
house Haus
hungry hungrig

I

ice cream Eis
idea Idee
India Indien
into in (... hinein)
invitation Einladung
island Insel

J

jam Marmelade
January Januar
jeans Jeans
juggler Jongleur/in
juice Saft
July Juli
jump up aufspringen
June Juni

K

keyboard 1. Keyboard,
  2. Tastatur
king König
kitchen Küche
knee Knie
know wissen

L

leaf, leaves Blatt, Blätter
left links
leg Bein
lemon Zitrone
lettuce Salat
light hell, leicht
like mögen
lion Löwe
living room Wohnzimmer
long lang
look schauen
love lieben

M

March März
May Mai
milk Milch
mobile phone Handy
Monday Montag
monkey Affe
*****monster** Monster
morning Morgen
mother Mutter
motorbike Motorrad
mountain Berg
mouse 1. Maus,
  2. Computermaus
mouth Mund
mud Schlamm
*****mushroom** Pilz

N

name Name
nature Natur
need brauchen
nice nett
no nein
nose Nase
notebook 1. Notizbuch,
  2. Notebook
November November
now jetzt
number Nummer,
  nummerieren

O

o'clock Uhr
October Oktober
old alt
on auf
open offen, öffnen
orange 1. orange,
  2. Apfelsine
orange juice Orangensaft

P

paper Papier
parrot Papagei
party Party, Feier
pen Füller, Stift
pencil Bleistift
pencil case Federmappe
pencil sharpener
  Anspitzer
photo Foto
picnic Picknick
picture Bild
plane Flugzeug
please bitte
popcorn Popcorn
poster Poster
present Geschenk
prince Prinz
pullover Pullover
purple lila
put setzen, stellen, legen
puzzle Puzzle

Q

queen Königin
quickly schnell

Word list

R

radio Radio
rainbow Regenbogen
rainy regnerisch
reach for greifen nach
red rot
right rechts
ringmaster
  Zirkusdirektor/in
river Fluss
robot Roboter
*****rose** Rose
round rund
rubber Radiergummi
ruler Lineal

S

sad traurig
sandwich Sandwich
Saturday Samstag
*****sausage** Würstchen
say sagen
scarf Halstuch, Schal
scissors Schere
scoop Eiskugel
see sehen
September September
shelf Regal
ship Schiff
shirt Hemd
shoe Schuh
shop Geschäft
shorts kurze Hose
shoulder Schulter
sing singen
sister Schwester
sit down sich hinsetzen
skateboard Skateboard
skeleton Skelett
*****skipping** Seilspringen
sky Himmel
small klein
snake Schlange
snowdrop Schnee-
  glöckchen
snowman Schneemann
snowy verschneit
sock Socke
some etwas
sour sauer
South Africa Südafrika

speak sprechen
spring Frühling
stamp aufstampfen
stand 1. Stand, 2. stehen
stand up aufstehen
start Anfang, Start
station Bahnhof
step Schritt
stepbrother Stiefbruder
stepmother Stiefmutter
stepsister Stiefschwester
stocking Strumpf
*****stone** Stein
storeroom Vorratsraum
story Geschichte
strawberry Erdbeere
street Straße
suitcase Koffer
summer Sommer
Sunday Sonntag
sunny sonnig
sweet süß

T

T-shirt T-Shirt
table Tisch
take nehmen
take a card eine Karte
  ziehen / nehmen
tasty lecker
*****tea** Tee
teacher Lehrer/in
telephone Telefon
telephone call Anruf
thirsty durstig
through durch
Thursday Donnerstag
tightrope walker
  Seiltänzer/in
time Zeit
toaster Toaster
today heute
toe Zeh
tomato Tomate
touch berühren
train Zug
tree Baum
Tuesday Dienstag
tummy Bauch
tuna Thunfisch
turn drehen

turn around sich
  umdrehen
TV Fernseher

U

under unter
up auf, hinauf
USA Vereinigte Staaten
  von Amerika

V

vampire Vampir
vanilla Vanille
vehicle Fahrzeug

W

walk laufen, spazieren
  gehen
want wollen
wardrobe Kleiderschrank
warm warm
wash waschen, spülen
washing machine
  Waschmaschine
water Wasser
wear anhaben, tragen
weather Wetter
Wednesday Mittwoch
welcome willkommen
what was
when wann
white weiß
wiggle hin und her
  bewegen, zappeln
window 1. Fenster,
  2. Bildschirmfenster
windy windig
winner Gewinner
winter Winter
wish Wunsch
witch Hexe
wolf Wolf
wrong falsch

Y

year Jahr
yellow gelb
yes ja

*Wörter von den Spotlight-
Seiten